I Can Listen to English! 1

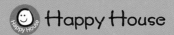
Happy House

Dear Teachers and Parents,

Welcome to Happy House **"I Can Listen to English!"**

Happy House Listening is designed to meet the needs and interests of children. It aims to help children develop and improve the listening skills necessary to communicate in a fun environment. The full-color illustrations are based on a creative storyline that includes funny characters like Toby and Cory, elves who live in the attic. The fantastic story encourages children to build their English listening skills. Happy House Listening is a three-level course containing 10 units, and after every five units, four-page reviews for each level. Each unit features a question and an answer with 8~10 alternative words. A topic which draws on the everyday lives and experiences of children with a fun story has been added. This book is child-centered in order to benefit young children and to prepare them for the fruitful use of English listening at a higher level.

● E2K Contents

A creative group that provides quality contents and educational services in English for ESL and EFL students.
The goal of E2K is to make the finest quality materials to make learning English more enjoyable for students.

TABLE OF CONTENTS

How to Use This Book --- 4

UNIT 01 It's an Apple Fruits & Vegetables ------------------- 7

UNIT 02 I Am Six Years Old Numbers -------------------- 13

UNIT 03 It's Red Colors --- 19

UNIT 04 I Have a Pencil Stationery --------------------- 25

UNIT 05 I Want Pizza Foods --------------------------------- 31

REVIEW 1 (UNITS 1~5) -------------------------------------- 37

UNIT 06 I Like Monkeys Animals ------------------------- 41

UNIT 07 It's Monday Days of the Week --------------------- 47

UNIT 08 I'm Playing Actions --------------------------------- 53

UNIT 09 It's Sunny Weather ------------------------------- 59

UNIT 10 He's My Father Family Members ------------------- 65

REVIEW 2 (UNITS 6~10) -------------------------------------- 71

Chant List -- 75

Stickers for Speak & Play ------------------------------------- 82

HOW TO USE
"I CAN LISTEN TO ENGLISH!"

Chant Listening

It helps to present new structures and new words in a fun and easy way. And it also provides motivation for listening.

Sentence Listening

This listening exercise reinforces the previous pages to help students learn sentence structures.

Word Listening

This listening exercise provides thorough practice in using new words.

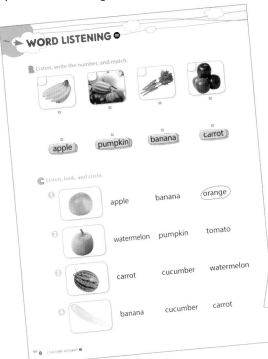

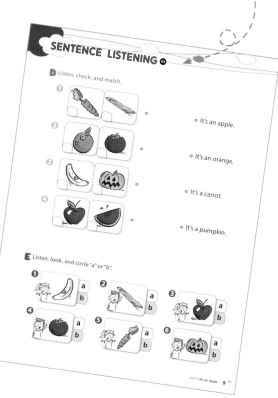

Speak & Play

This oral activity encourages communication by playing a game.

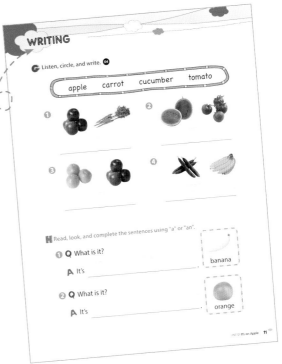

Writing

These listening activities give learners the opportunity to practice structures and words by writing.

Phonics Listening

This phonics story gives learners the chance to read short stories. This listening and writing activity contains questions designed to improve students' understanding of phonics rules.

Review

These are systematic recycling and review pages.

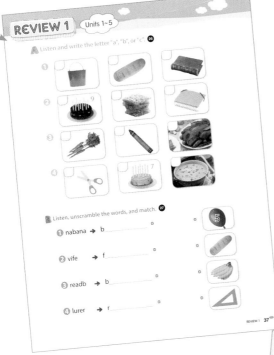

Phonics Review

The various questions in this section help learners to understand phonics rules and improve their listening, reading, and writing skills. They also help increase learners' vocabularies.

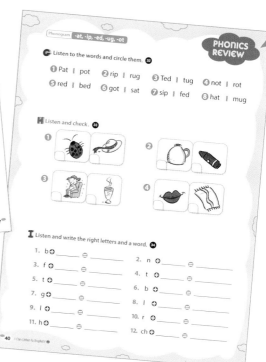

UNIT 01

It's an Apple

CHANT LISTENING 01

A Listen and chant.
Then circle the fruits and the vegetables you hear in the chant.

B Listen, write the number, and match.

○ ○ ○ ○

○ ○ ○ ○

(apple)　(pumpkin)　(banana)　(carrot)

C Listen, look, and circle.

❶ 　apple　banana　(orange)

❷ 　watermelon　pumpkin　tomato

❸ 　carrot　cucumber　watermelon

❹ 　banana　cucumber　carrot

D Listen, check, and match.

1. ○   ○ It's an apple.

2. ○   ○ It's an orange.

3. ○   ○ It's a carrot.

4. ○   ○ It's a pumpkin.

E Listen, look, and circle "a" or "b".

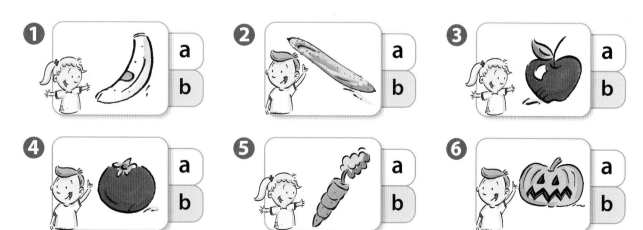

1. a / b
2. a / b
3. a / b
4. a / b
5. a / b
6. a / b

SPEAK & PLAY

F Ask and answer with your partner. Follow the steps below.

What is it?

It's a/an _____.

apple   tomato   orange
banana   carrot   pumpkin
watermelon   cucumber

Step 1. Find a partner.

Step 2. Your partner asks you a question, and then you answer it.

Step 3. Find the Fruit or Vegetable Sticker for your answer.

Step 4. Attach the sticker on the basket.

WRITING

Listen, circle, and write. **04**

> apple   carrot   cucumber   tomato

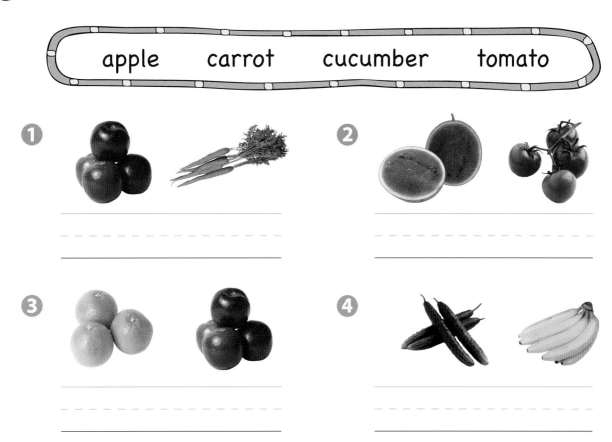

① _____
   _____

② _____
   _____

③ _____
   _____

④ _____
   _____

H Read, look, and complete the sentences using "a" or "an".

① **Q** What is it?

   A It's _____ .

banana

② **Q** What is it?

   A It's _____ .

orange

I Listen and read the phonics story.

Pat on the mat.
Cat on the hat.
Zat on the mat.
Bat on the hat.

What is it?
What is it?
A rat.
It's a rat.

J Listen and write the right letters and a word.

cat   bat   hat   Pat   rat   mat

1. b ⊕ _____at_____ ⊖ _____bat_____
2. c ⊕ _____ ⊖ _____

3. h ⊕ _____ ⊖ _____
4. P ⊕ _____ ⊖ _____

5. r ⊕ _____ ⊖ _____
6. m ⊕ _____ ⊖ _____

I'm Six Years Old

CHANT LISTENING 06

A Listen and chant.
Then circle the numbers you hear in the chant.

WORD LISTENING 07

B Listen, circle, and match.

1   ○ ○ five

2   ○ ○ six

3    ○ ○ eight

4    ○ ○ two

C Listen, check, and circle the word.

1

ten | nine

2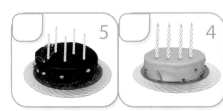

four | five

3

two | one

4

three | seven

SENTENCE LISTENING 08

D Listen, check, and match.

1 9 / 4 ○　　　○ I'm five years old.

2 8 / 5 ○　　　○ I'm nine years old.

3 6 / 7 ○　　　○ I'm seven years old.

4 3 / 5 ○　　　○ I'm eight years old.

E Listen, look, and circle "a" or "b".

1  a b

2  a b

3  a b

4  a b

5  a b

6  a b

SPEAK & PLAY

F Ask and answer with your partner. Follow the steps below.

How old are you?

I'm _____ years old.

three   four   five
six   seven   eight
nine   ten

Step 1. 🖐 Find a partner. Step 2. 🖐 Your partner asks you a question, and then you answer it.

Step 3. 🖐 Find the Number and Word Sticker for your answer.

Step 4. 🖐 Attach the Number sticker to a circle and then attach the word sticker to the right rectang

WRITING

G Listen, circle, and write. **09**

seven   nine   one   five

1

_____

2

_____

3

_____

4

_____

H Read, look, and complete the sentences using "years".

1 Q How old are you?

A I'm _____ old.

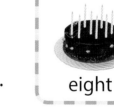

eight

2 Q How old are you?

A I'm _____ old.

six

PHONICS LISTENING 🔟

Phonogram **-ip**

I Listen and read the phonics story.

Big lips.
Sip some coke.
Big chips.
Rip some snacks.

How old are you?
I'm six years old.

J Listen and write the right words.

chip	rip	zip	sip	tip	lip

1. _____ some water

2. big _____ s

3. _____ some paper

4. _____ it up

5. _____ the man

6. small _____ s

UNIT 03

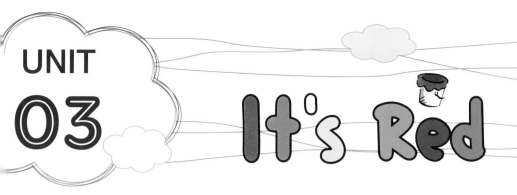

It's Red

A Listen and chant.
Then circle the colors you hear in the chant.

B Listen, write the number, and match.

○   ○   ○   ○

○   ○   ○   ○

green   red   blue   yellow

C Listen, look, and circle.

1    pink   red   brown

2    yellow   blue   pink

3    black   brown   blue

4    pink   purple   red

D Listen, check, and match.

1. ▫ · It's blue.

2. ▫ · It's yellow.

3. ▫ · It's pink.

4. ▫ · It's brown.

E Listen, look, and circle "a" or "b".

1. a / b

2. a / b

3. a / b

4. a / b

5. a / b

6. a / b

SPEAK & PLAY

F Ask and answer with your partner. Follow the steps below.

What color is it?

It's _____.

red	yellow	green
blue	pink	black
purple	brown	

Step 1. Find a partner.

Step 2. Your partner asks you a question, and then you answer it.

Step 3. Find the color of 8 crayons, and then paint the colors.

WRITING

G Listen, circle, and write. 🔴14

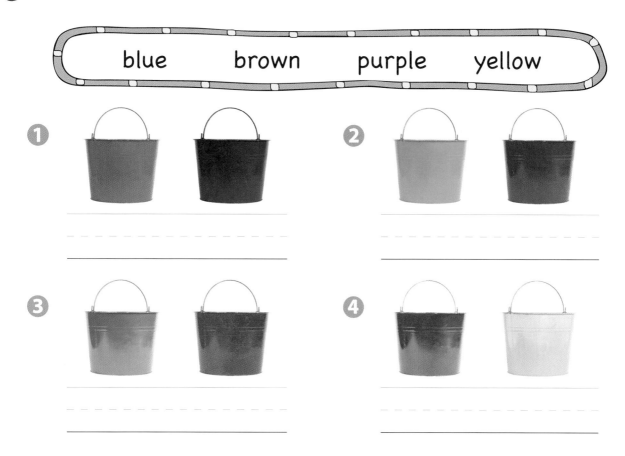

blue   brown   purple   yellow

① ② ③ ④

H Read, look, and complete the sentences.

① Q What color is it?

A It's _____ .

green

② Q What color is it?

A It's _____ .

red

I Listen and read the phonics story.

Ted in bed.
Ned in bed.
Mom fed Ted.
Mom fed Ned.

What color?
What color is it?
It's red.
It's a red bed.

J Listen and write the right letters and a word.

red   bed   Ted   fed   Ned

1. T ➕ _____ ⊜ _____

2. r ➕ _____ ⊜ _____

3. _____ ➕ ed ⊜ _____

4. b ➕ _____ ⊜ _____

5. N ➕ _____ ⊜ _____

6. _____ ➕ ed ⊜ _____

UNIT 04

I Have a Pencil

CHANT LISTENING 16

A Listen and chant.
Then circle the stationery you hear in the chant.

B Listen, circle, and match.

①  ○ ○ crayon

② ○ ○ book

③ ○ ○ pencil

④ ○ ○ scissors

⑤ ○ ○ eraser

C Listen, check, and circle the word.

①

pen ┃ crayon

②

notebook ┃ pencil

③

ruler ┃ scissors

④

eraser ┃ book

D Listen, check, and match.

1. ○   ○ I have a ruler.

2. ○   ○ I have scissors.

3. ○   ○ I have a pen.

4. ○   ○ I have a notebook.

E Listen, look, and circle "a" or "b".

1  a b

2  a b

3  a b

4  a b

5  a b

6  a b

SPEAK & PLAY

F Ask and answer with your partner. Follow the steps below.

What do you have?

I have _____.

a book   a notebook   a pen
a pencil   a crayon   a ruler
an eraser   scissors

Let's go~!!

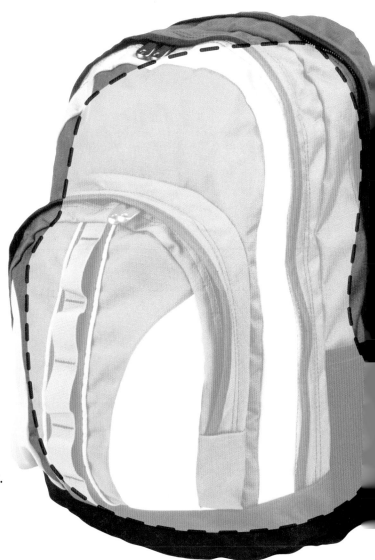

Step 1. Find a partner.

Step 2. Your partner asks you a question, and then you answer it.

Step 3. Find the Word Sticker for your answer.

Step 4. Attach the sticker to the backpack.

WRITING

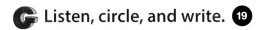

Listen, circle, and write. 🔟

| notebook | pencil | ruler | scissors |

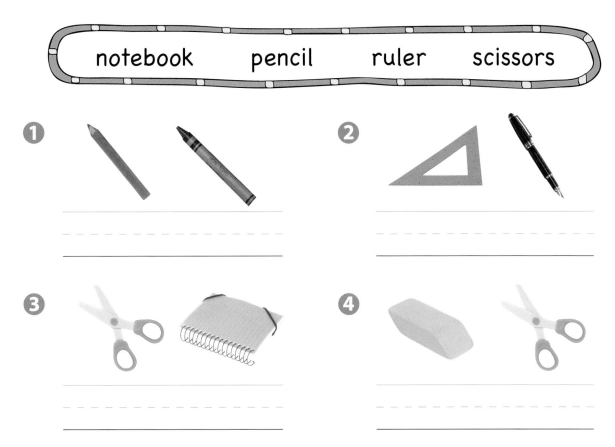

①

②

③

④

H Read, look, and complete the sentences using "a" or "an".

① **Q** What do you have?

A I have _____ .

eraser

② **Q** What do you have?

A I have _____ .

crayon

PHONICS LISTENING ⑳

I Listen and read the phonics story.

Bugs under the rug.
Bugs in the jug.
Tug the bugs.
Lug the bugs.

What do they have?
Mug. A mug.
They have a mug.

J Listen and write the right words.

| rug | lug | mug | bug | jug | tug |

1. _____ the bag

2. _____s under the bed

3. my _____

4. _____ the bugs

5. a red _____

6. water in the _____

I Want Pizza

CHANT LISTENING 21

A Listen and chant.
Then circle the foods you hear in the chant.

LUNCH SPECIAL "PIZZA"

MILK

orange juice

B Listen, write the number, and match.

noodles   rice   bread   juice

C Listen, look, and circle.

1    milk   juice   rice

2    bread   pizza   noodles

3    rice   soup   chicken

4    soup   juice   milk

SENTENCE LISTENING ㉓

D Listen, check, and match.

1 ○ ○ I want rice.

2 ○ ○ I want bread.

3 ○ ○ I want juice.

4 ○ ○ I want soup.

E Listen, look, and circle "a" or "b".

1  a / b

2  a / b

3  a / b

4  a / b

5  a / b

6  a / b

SPEAK & PLAY

F Ask and answer with your partner. Follow the steps below.

What do you want?

I want _____ .

pizza	chicken	soup
rice	noodles	milk
juice	bread	

Step 1. Find a partner. **Step 2.** Your partner asks you a question, and then you answer

Step 3. Find the Food Sticker for your answer.

Step 4. Attach the sticker to the dish.

WRITING

G Listen, circle, and write. 24

noodles   chicken   bread   juice

1 _____

2 _____

3 _____

4 _____

H Read, look, and complete the sentences.

1 **Q** What do you want?

   A I want _____ .

soup

2 **Q** What do you want?

   A I want _____ .

milk

I Listen and read the phonics story.

Not the hot soup.
Not the hot rice.
Got the hot pizza.
Got the hot meat.

What do you want?
I want a hot hotdog.

J Listen and write the right letters and a word.

| tot | pot | hot | got | not | dot |

1. h ➕ ___ → _____ meat

2. n ➕ ___ → _____ the hot so

3. g ➕ ___ → _____ the hot rice

4. p ➕ ___ → a big _____

5. d ➕ ___ → a small _____

6. t ➕ ___ → a tiny _____

REVIEW 1 Units 1~5

A Listen and write the letter "a", "b", or "c". 26

①

②

③

④

B Listen, unscramble the words, and match. 27

① nabana ➜ b_____ ○

② vife ➜ f_____ ○

③ readb ➜ b_____ ○

④ lurer ➜ r_____ ○

Listen and match. 28

1
What color is it? ○   ○ I want pizza.

2
How old are you? ○   ○ It's red.

3
What do you want? ○   ○ I have a crayon.

4
What is it? ○   ○ I'm three years old.

5
What do you have? ○   ○ It's a carrot.

D **Listen, find the picture, and write the number.** 29

E Listen, write the number, and match. **30**

[ ] What is it? ∘	∘ I have two books.
[ ] What do you want? ∘	∘ I want a green apple.
[ ] What do you have? ∘	∘ I am nine.
[ ] How old are you? ∘	∘ It is a pencil.

F Listen, look, and complete the sentences. **31**

carrots   crayon   four   juice   orange   yellow

1

Q What is it?

A It is a _____ _____.

2

Q What do you have?

A I have _____ _____.

3

Q What do you want?

A I want _____ _____.

G Listen to the words and circle them. **32**

1 Pat ❙ pot   2 rip ❙ rug   3 Ted ❙ tug   4 not ❙ rot

5 red ❙ bed   6 got ❙ sat   7 sip ❙ fed   8 hat ❙ mug

H Listen and check. **33**

1

2

3

4

I Listen and write the right letters and a word. **34**

1. b ✚ _____ ⊖ _____   2. n ✚ _____ ⊖ _____

3. f ✚ _____ ⊖ _____   4. t ✚ _____ ⊖ _____

5. t ✚ _____ ⊖ _____   6. b ✚ _____ ⊖ _____

7. g ✚ _____ ⊖ _____   8. l ✚ _____ ⊖ _____

9. l ✚ _____ ⊖ _____   10. r ✚ _____ ⊖ _____

11. h ✚ _____ ⊖ _____   12. ch ✚ _____ ⊖ _____

UNIT 06

I Like Monkeys

CHANT LISTENING 35

A Listen and chant.
Then circle the animals you hear in the chant.

B Listen, circle, and match.

1 ○ ○ dolphin

2 ○ ○ giraffe

3 ○ ○ monkey

4 ○ ○ bird

5 ○ ○ penguin

C Listen, check, and circle the word.

1

zebras | monkeys

2

lions | dolphins

3

bears | birds

4

penguins | giraffes

D Listen, check, and match.

① I like monkeys.

② I like lions.

③ I like penguins.

④ I like dolphins.

E Listen, look, and circle "a" or "b".

① a b

② a b

③ a b

④ a b

⑤ a b

⑥ a b

SPEAK & PLAY

F Ask and answer with your partner. Follow the steps below.

What animals do you like?

I like _____.

bears   lions   zebras
giraffes dolphins penguins
birds   monkeys

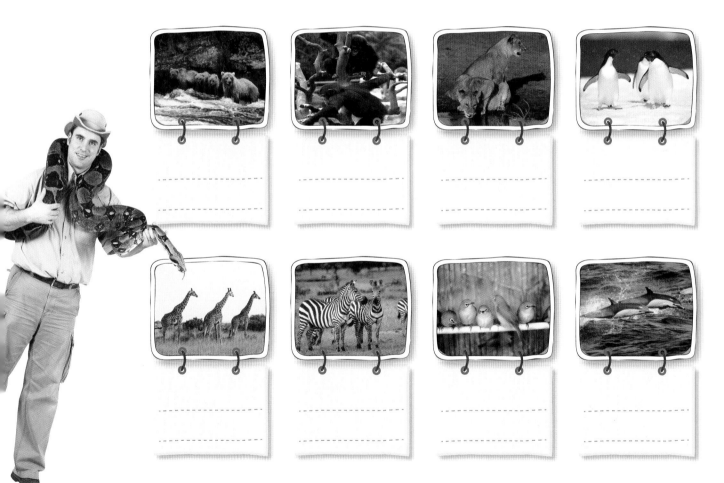

Step 1. 🖐 Show the pictures above to your friends.

Step 2. 🖐 Ask your friends the question above.

Step 3. 🖐 After getting the answers to the question, write your friends' names below the pictures of the animals.

WRITING

Listen, circle, and write. **38**

| zebra | giraffe | penguin | dolphin |

1

_____

2

_____

3

_____

4

_____

H Read, look, and complete the sentences.

1 Q What animals do you like?

A I like _____ .

birds

2 Q What animals do you like?

A I like _____ .

monkeys

I Listen and read the phonics story.

Ben likes pens.
What about Ken?

What animals do you like?
I like hens.
Ken likes hens, too.
Here are ten hens.

MAGIC SHOW!

Ben

Ken

J Listen and write the right letters and a word.

hen   Ben   pen   ten   Ken

1. p ➕ _____ ➖ _____

2. _____ ➕ en ➖ _____

3. _____ ➕ en ➖ _____

4. t ➕ _____ ➖ _____

5. _____ ➕ en ➖ _____

It's Monday

CHANT LISTENING 40

A Listen and chant.
Then circle the days of the week you hear in the chant.

WORD LISTENING 🔵41

B Listen, write the number, and match.

MON   SUN   THU   TUE

Thursday   Monday   Tuesday   Sunday

C Listen, look, and circle.

❶ [Week] Sunday Monday Tuesday / Wednesday Thursday Friday (?)

Saturday   Sunday   Monday

❷ [Week] Sunday Monday Tuesday / (?) Thursday Friday Saturday

Tuesday   Wednesday   Friday

❸ [Week] Sunday Monday Tuesday / Wednesday Thursday (?) Saturday

Thursday   Friday   Sunday

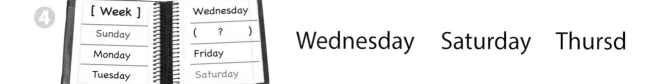

❹ [Week] Sunday Monday Tuesday / Wednesday (?) Friday Saturday

Wednesday   Saturday   Thursd

D Listen, check, and match.

1 ○   ○ It's Monday.

2 ○   ○ It's Tuesday.

3 ○   ○ It's Thursday.

4 ○   ○ It's Sunday.

E Listen, look, and circle "a" or "b".

1 a / b

2 a / b

3 a / b

4 a / b

5 a / b

6 a / b

SPEAK & PLAY

F Ask and answer with your partner. Follow the steps below.

What day is it?

It's _____.

Sunday   Monday   Tuesday
Wednesday   Thursday
Friday   Saturday

Step 1. Find a partner.

Step 2. Your partner asks you a question, and then you answer it.

Step 3. Find the Word Sticker for your answer.

Step 4. Attach the day sticker to the blackboard.

WRITING

G Listen, circle, and write. 43

Wednesday   Friday   Saturday   Thursday

1

_____

2

_____

3

_____

4

_____

H Read, look, and complete the sentences.

1 Q What day is it?

A It's _____ .

2 Q What day is it?

A It's _____ .

I Listen and read the phonics story.

What day is it?
It's Monday.

Sam eats ham.
Pam eats jam.
The ram eats yams.

Today is Monday.
Today is ham, jam,
and yam eating day!

J Listen and write the right words.

Jam   Pam   yam   ham   Sam   ram

1. _____ eats rice.

2. _____ is good.

3. Sam eats _____.

4. The _____ eats pizza.

5. The ram eats _____s.

6. _____ is nice.

I'm Playing

CHANT LISTENING 45

A Listen and chant.
Then circle the actions you hear in the chant.

B Listen, circle, and match.

1    listening

2   reading

3   singing

4    eating

5   climbing

C Listen, check, and circle the word.

1
reading | running

2
jumping | listening

3
singing | playing

4
climbing | playing

SENTENCE LISTENING 🔊47

D Listen, check, and match.

1. 　　　○　　　　○ I'm singing.

2.　　　　　　　　　　　　○　　　　○ I'm reading.

3.　　　　　　　　　　　　○　　　　○ I'm eating.

4.　　　　　　　　　　　　○　　　　○ I'm listening.

E Listen, look, and circle "a" or "b".

1  a / b

2  a / b

3  a / b

4  a / b

5  a / b

6  a / b

SPEAK & PLAY

F Ask and answer with your partner. Follow the steps below.

What are you doing?  I'm _____.

climbing   eating   jumping
reading   singing   listening
playing   running

Step 1. 🖐 Find a partner. Step 2. 🖐 Your partner asks you a question, and then you answer it.

Step 3. 🖐 Find the sticker for your answer.

Step 4. 🖐 Attach the sticker below the right picture on the blackboard.

WRITING

G Listen, circle, and write. **48**

> climbing   singing   running   listening

1 _____

2 _____

3 _____

4 _____

H Read, look, and complete the sentences.

1 Q What are you doing?

A I'm _____ .

eating

2 Q What are you doing?

A I'm _____ .

reading

PHONICS LISTENING 🔵49

Phonogram **-op**

I Listen and read the phonics story.

A boy pops the corn.
A boy mops the floor.
A girl spins the top.
A girl sops some bread.

What are you doing?
Hop. Hopping.
I'm hopping.

J Listen and write the right letters and a word.

pop   mop   top   sop   hop

1. t ⊕ _____ ⊖ _____   **2.** _____ ⊕ op ⊖ _____

3. s ⊕ _____ ⊖ _____   **4.** _____ ⊕ op ⊖ _____

5. m ⊕ _____ ⊖ _____

UNIT 09

It's Sunny

CHANT LISTENING 50

A Listen and chant.
Then circle the weather conditions you hear in the chant.

WORD LISTENING 🔵51

B Listen, write the number, and match.

 snowy   rainy   cloudy   sunny

C Listen, look, and circle.

①    rainy   windy   snowy

②    foggy   snowy   sunny

③    sunny   stormy   snowy

④   foggy   thundering   stormy

D Listen, check, and match.

1    ○   ○ It's rainy.

2    ○   ○ It's foggy.

3    ○   ○ It's sunny.

4    ○   ○ It's windy.

E Listen, look, and circle "a" or "b".

1  a b

2  a b

3  a b

4  a b

5  a b

6  a b

SPEAK & PLAY

F Ask and answer with your partner. Follow the steps below.

How's the weather?

It's _____.

sunny   rainy   snowy
foggy   windy   thundering
stormy   cloudy

sunny

rainy

snowy

foggy

windy

thundering

stormy

cloudy

Step 1. Find a partner. **Step 2.** Your partner asks you a question, and then you answer it.

Step 3. Find the Weather Sticker for your answer.

Step 4. Attach the sticker over the right word on the TV.

WRITING

G Listen, circle, and write. **53**

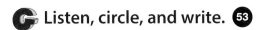

cloudy   foggy   snowy   thundering

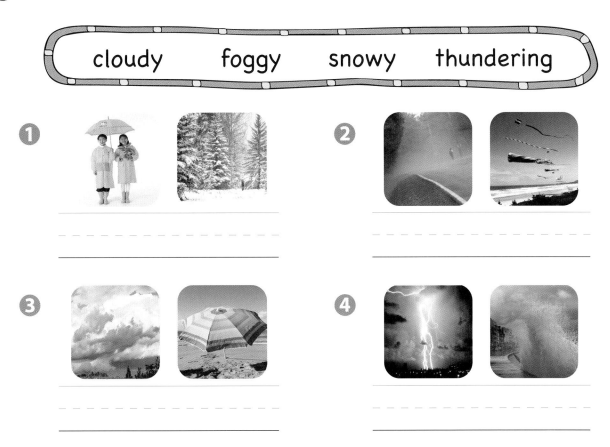

1

2

3

4

H Read, look, and complete the sentences.

1 Q How's the weather?

A It's _____ .

rainy

2 Q How's the weather?

A It's _____ .

sunny

Phonogram **-un**

I Listen and read the phonics story.

Fun with buns.
Run with me.

Fun in the sun.
How's the weather?
Sunny. It's sunny.

J Listen and write the right words.

| bun | Run | sun | fun |

1. _____ with Tom.

2. This is _____ .

3. He eats _____ s.

4. It's the red _____ .

UNIT 10

He's My Father

CHANT LISTENING 55

A Listen and chant.
Then circle the family members you hear in the chant.

Shawn's Family Tree

Grandfather	Grandmother

Mother | Father | Uncle | Aunt

Shawn | Sister | Baby brother

WORD LISTENING 56

B Listen, circle, and match.

1 (brother) (uncle) (aunt) ∘

2 (sister) (father) (mother) ∘

3 (uncle) (grandfather) (brother) ∘

4 (brother) (sister) (aunt) ∘

C Listen, check, and circle the word.

1

aunt | uncle

2

brother | father

3

grandfather | grandmother

4

mother | sister

D Listen, check, and match.

1 ○ ○ She's my sister.

2 ○ ○ He's my brother.

3 ○ ○ She's my aunt.

4 ○ ○ He's my uncle.

E Listen, look, and circle "a" or "b".

1  a / b

2  a / b

3  a / b

4  a / b

5  a / b

6  a / b

SPEAK & PLAY

F Ask and answer with your partner. Follow the steps below.

Who is he/she?

He's/She's my
_____.

grandfather   grandmother
father   mother   brother
sister   uncle   aunt

Shawn's Family Tree

Shawn   Baby brother

Step 1. 🖐 Find a partner.

Step 2. 🖐 You are "Shawn". Your partner asks you a question, and then you answer it.

Step 3. 🖐 Find the Word Sticker for your answer.

Step 4. 🖐 Attach the sticker below the right picture on the family tree.

WRITING

 Listen, circle, and write. 58

```
brother    grandmother    sister    uncle
```

1

_____

2

_____

3

_____

4

_____

 Read, look, and complete the sentences using "my".

1 **Q** Who is he?

A He's _____ .

father

2 **Q** Who is she?

A She's _____ .

aunt

I Listen and read the phonics story.

A boy sits on the kit.
A boy fits in his pants.
A boy hits the ball.
A boy bit an apple.

Who is he?
Brother. My brother.
He's my brother.

Who is he?

J Listen and write the right letters and a word.

hit   bit   fit   kit   sit

1. h ✚ _____ ➖ _____

2. _____ ✚ it ➖ _____

3. _____ ✚ it ➖ _____

4. f ✚ _____ ➖ _____

5. b ✚ _____ ➖ _____

6. _____ ✚ it ➖ _____

Listen and write the letter "a", "b", or "c". 60

①

②

③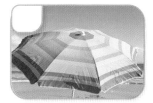

④

 Listen, unscramble the words, and match. 61

① loudcy ➜ c_____ ○   ○

② azbre ➜ z_____ ○   ○

③ yadrFi ➜ F_____ ○   ○

④ uclne ➜ u_____ ○   ○

C Listen and match. 🔢62

1  What day is it? ○   ○ I'm singing.

2 How's the weather? ○   ○ He's my father.

3 What are you doing? ○   ○ It's snowy.

4 Who is he? ○   ○ I like giraffes.

5 What animals do you like? ○   ○ It's Sunday.

D Listen, find the picture, and write the number. 🔢63

E Listen, write the number, and match. 🔵64

☐	What is he doing?	○ ○	I'm Shawn.
☐	Who are you?	○ ○	He's reading.
☐	How's the weather?	○ ○	Today is Tuesday.
☐	What day is it today?	○ ○	It's rainy.

F Listen, look, and complete the sentences. 🔵65

lions   grandmother   like   my   jumping

❶

Q Who is she?

A She's _____ _____.

❷

Q What animals do you like?

A I _____ _____.

❸

Q What is she doing?

A She's _____.

G Listen to the words and circle them. **66**

1 ten | top   2 run | ham   3 bit | Ben   4 Pam | pen

5 bun | fit   6 pop | fun   7 sun | sop   8 hit | hen

H Listen and check. **67**

I Listen and write the right letters and a word. **68**

1. t ⊕ _____ ⊜ _____   2. h ⊕ _____ ⊜ _____

3. b ⊕ _____ ⊜ _____   4. b ⊕ _____ ⊜ _____

5. S ⊕ _____ ⊜ _____   6. K ⊕ _____ ⊜ _____

7. f ⊕ _____ ⊜ _____   8. s ⊕ _____ ⊜ _____

9. k ⊕ _____ ⊜ _____   10. y ⊕ _____ ⊜ _____

11. p ⊕ _____ ⊜ _____   12. r ⊕ _____ ⊜ _____

CHANT LIST

Unit 1 **It's an Apple**  Page 7

What is it? What is it?

Apple. Apple. It's an apple.

What is it? What is it?

Banana. Banana. It's a banana.

What is it? What is it?

Orange. Orange. It's an orange.

What is it? What is it?

Watermelon. Watermelon. It's a watermelon.

What is it? What is it?

Carrot. Carrot. It's a carrot.

What is it? What is it?

Tomato. Tomato. It's a tomato.

What is it? What is it?

Pumpkin. Pumpkin. It's a pumpkin.

What is it? What is it?

Cucumber. Cucumber. It's a cucumber.

How old are you? How old are you?
I'm six. I'm six years old.
How old are you? How old are you?
I'm five. I'm five years old.
How old are you? How old are you?
I'm eight. I'm eight years old.

How old are you? How old are you?
I'm seven. I'm seven years old.
How old are you? How old are you?
I'm four. I'm four years old.
How old are you? How old are you?
I'm three. I'm three years old.

What color is it?
It's red. Its color is red.
What color is it?
It's blue. Its color is blue.
What color is it?
It's green. Its color is green.
What color is it?
It's yellow. Its color is yellow.

What color is it?
It's brown. Its color is brown.
What color is it?
It's pink. Its color is pink.
What color is it?
It's black. Its color is black.
What color is it?
It's purple. Its color is purple.

Unit 4　I Have a Pencil

What do you have? What do you have?
I have a pencil. Pencil. Pencil. Pencil.
I have a book. Book. Book. Book.
I have an eraser. Eraser. Eraser. Eraser.
I have a notebook. Notebook. Notebook. Notebook.

What do you have? What do you have?
I have a ruler. Ruler. Ruler. Ruler.
I have a pen. Pen. Pen. Pen.
I have a crayon. Crayon. Crayon. Crayon.
I have scissors. Scissors. Scissors. Scissors.

Unit 5　I Want Pizza
Page 31

What do you want? What do you want?
Pizza. Pizza. I want pizza.
Rice. Rice. I want rice.
What do you want? What do you want?
Noodles. Noodles. I want noodles.
Chicken. Chicken. I want chicken.

What do you want? What do you want?
Bread. Bread. I want bread.
Milk. Milk. I want milk.
What do you want? What do you want?
Soup. Soup. I want soup.
Juice. Juice. I want juice.

77

Animals. Animals. What animals do you like?
Monkeys. Monkeys. I like monkeys.
Animals. Animals. What animals do you like?
Bears. Bears. I like bears.
Animals. Animals. What animals do you like?
Lions. Lions. I like lions.
Animals. Animals. What animals do you like?
Penguins. Penguins. I like penguins.
Animals. Animals. What animals do you like?
Giraffes. Giraffes. I like giraffes.
Animals. Animals. What animals do you like?
Zebras. Zebras. I like zebras.
Animals. Animals. What animals do you like?
Birds. Birds. I like birds.
Animals. Animals. What animals do you like?
Dolphins. Dolphins. I like dolphins.

What day is it?
It's Sunday! Day. Day. It's Sunday!
What day is it?
It's Monday! Day. Day. It's Monday!
What day is it?
It's Tuesday! Day. Day. It's Tuesday!
What day is it?
It's Wednesday! Day. Day. It's Wednesday!
What day is it?
It's Thursday! Day. Day. It's Thursday!
What day is it?
It's Friday! Day. Day. It's Friday!
What day is it?
It's Saturday! Day. Day. It's Saturday!
Sunday, Monday, Tuesday, Wednesday, Thursday, Friday, Saturday!

Unit 8 | I'm Playing Page 53

What, what are you doing?
I'm playing. Playing. Playing.
What, what are you doing?
I'm running. Running. Running.
What, what are you doing?
I'm jumping. Jumping. Jumping.
What, what are you doing?
I'm climbing. Climbing. Climbing.
Playing. Running. Jumping. Climbing.

What, what are you doing?
I'm eating. Eating. Eating.
What, what are you doing?
I'm reading. Reading. Reading.
What, what are you doing?
I'm singing. Singing. Singing.
What, what are you doing?
I'm listening. Listening. Listening.
Eating. Reading. Singing. Listening.

Unit 9 | It's Sunny Page 59

How's the weather? Weather. Weather.
Sunny. Sunny. It's sunny.
How's the weather? Weather. Weather.
Rainy. Rainy. It's rainy.
How's the weather? Weather. Weather.
Snowy. Snowy. It's snowy.
How's the weather? Weather. Weather.
Foggy. Foggy. It's foggy.
How's the weather? Weather. Weather.
Windy. Windy. It's windy.
How's the weather? Weather. Weather.

Cloudy. Cloudy. It's cloudy.
How's the weather? Weather. Weather.
Stormy. Stormy. It's stormy.
How's the weather? Weather. Weather.
Thundering. Thundering. It's thundering.

Unit 10 | He's My Father Page 65

Who is he? He, he?
Father. Father. He's my father.
Who is she? She, she?
Mother. Mother. She's my mother.
Who is he? He, he?
Grandfather. He's my grandfather.
Who is she? She, she?
Grandmother. She's my grandmother.

Who is he? He, he?
Brother. Brother. He's my baby brother.
Who is she? She, she?
Sister. Sister. She's my sister.
Who is he? He, he?
Uncle. Uncle. He's my uncle.
Who is she? She, she?
Aunt. Aunt. She's my aunt.

p.34

p.50

Sunday   Monday   Tuesday   Wednesday

Thursday   Friday   Saturday

p.56

climbing   eating   jumping   reading

singing   listening   playing   running

p.62

p.68

grandfather   grandmother   father

mother   sister   aunt   uncle

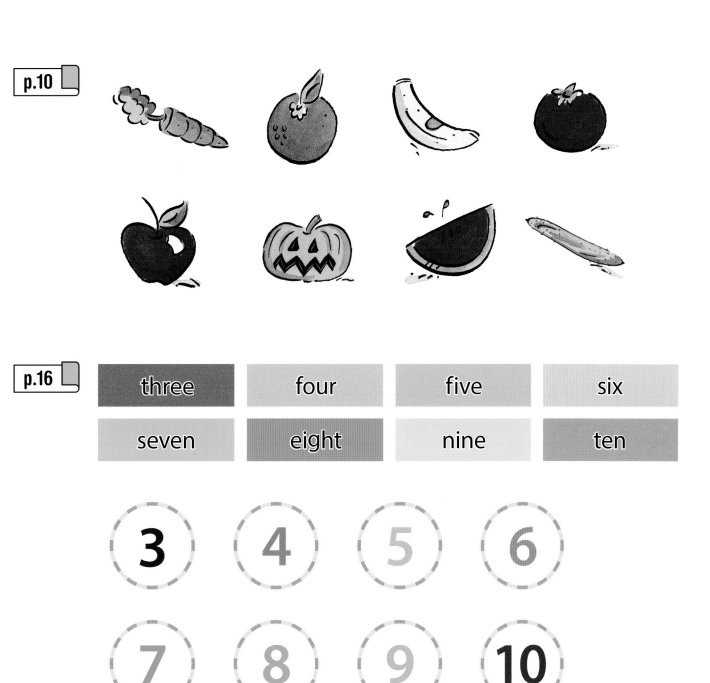

p.10

p.16

three	four	five	six
seven	eight	nine	ten

3   4   5   6

7   8   9   10

p.28

 book  notebook  pen  pencil

 crayon  ruler  eraser  scissors